Enchantment

Enchantment

Poems by

Kanchan Bhattacharya

Compiled by
Ms Tannaaz Irani
2015

PARTRIDGE
A Penguin Random House Company

To order additional copies of this book, contact
Partridge India
000 800 10062 62
orders.india@partridgepublishing.com

www.partridgepublishing.com/india

Contents

FOREWORD

This stirring collection of poems, is the third by Kanchan Bhattacharya, a versatile poet, who has been writing poetry ever his teens actually! A soulful poet, he has fans and followers across India and abroad, forever waiting for more from him!

This compilation has been divided into various sub-sections making it a complete poetic offering to any lover of ode and verse.

The Muse, as seen by Kanchan, is eternal, changing form, character and mood, light-hearted, mischievous, in darker shades, fanciful at times, harshly real when she wishes to be, hovering in the background at all times and yet ubiquitous. At times she personifies cannabis, or a nose! Sometimes, she prompts the poet into levity whence he delightfully presents nonsensical limericks! Oh, the Muse!

Pick your choice- from dark, forbidden, passionate love, or blatant carnality. This "In your face" quality of lustful, full-bodied love makes his poetry extremely powerful and leaves the reader shaken up, wanting more and more! He writes of women in all their desirability, in their myriad moods; in various avatars; as mistresses, lovers, wives; accompanied by erotic imagery.

Satiation is never a distant dream, when you read him!

Mumbai,   Tannaaz Irani
27 April 2015

ACKNOWLEDGEMENT

I am immensely indebted to MS Tannaaz Irani who has picked these poems from a manuscript of nearly 400 pages. Without her help, it would have been very difficult to progress the project all by myself.

And yes, there is Shaswati, my wife, who tends to my needs of tea coffee and plenty of TLC, and sometimes listens to my readings and tells me, no, this won't do, or you are good… and there is always tea… and she helped me to recover magically from the injuries in early June 2015.

Enchantment is thus dedicated to my wife, for all her patience. And thanks Tannaaz, you are good!

Last, but not the least, I am grateful to Partridge India, for taking up this project and progressing it so smoothly. Thanks, Mary Oxley.

Jabalpur- 22 Nov 2015   Kanchan

Preface

Every poem I write
Becomes a droplet of rain
From a night without end
In a black sky...

Every poem is a broken piece
Cast off from an ice pack
Of memories...

Every poem is a canopy
Of lies that I make up
To console my heart-
Not the feisty me,
A being of smiles
Walking about, head held high

Like the muddy river deluge that comes in monsoon floods, she has no home... her appearance is sudden, yet she leaves behind the alluvial deposits, the tender golden feeling that remains...

I have met her so many times in my life. She has always changed her form, and yet, retained the innocence of her childlike acceptance of me... to me, she appears simply as a woman/girl in need of a metaphorical home, permanence inside my heart. Like rain, she comes, like rain she goes away- a homeless child, a meandering dream, incomplete yet resonant.

Poetry is cyclical. My poetry is about the magic of phases in my life, the changes of the Muse. I speak of the voice inside me- and I wish to remain the poet of posthumous times... to be known when my last poem has been written!

As a child I thought I would die in water. As a fast ageing poet, I know it would be a merger, the sun glittering down the snow slopes, as I merge into the brilliance of the last noon… finally!

The Muse of liquid thoughts, Deirdre of the sorrow and grief, and the joys of Diane the Huntress, primal…

She is still the Muse, Eternity…

Jabalpur,   Kanchan Bhattacharya
27 April 2015

APHRODITE

To Aphrodite

Haiku
Darkness I forget-
Just soft words, some caresses,
Imprints eternal

Summer breeze, rains
In dark nights of loneliness,
You become my sleep

This heart like monsoon
Meanders gently, if you ask
I would stand quietly

The rain speaks, so hush
Your lips, serendipity
Passion, a river

I have sung for long
Now the void begins, you left
Your notes over me

Nimbus, nubile dream
On wings of a swallow, blues
So rare is this love

Aphrodite, spring forth,
The lei around lovers' waists
Kismet, your kisses

Symphony

On the dreamboat of desire
Packets of thoughts,
Little white wisps... clouds
In a blue sunlit sky,
Love is a bird, swallows in flight

The words are you
The soul is yours
Walk into the day
With a trail of fragrances,
The poet's passion follows you
In sunlight and rain
In dawns and sunsets
With zephyrs and gales
Through tornados and hail

Caresses from faraway
In midnight hours...
Sunlit and yet moon
On the fringe of kismet,
Your kisses still linger
A night of éclairs shared lip to lip
And wild fragrance of white roses
Just careless cadences
Of streaking meteorites
Of moans and touches
Seeking crescendos
Lost and found moments ago,
Not yet forgotten

Streaming exchanges, wilderness
Of caresses, from so far away
A journey often taken
Yet never before
Discovering new trekking tracks
On midnight lanes and rooms,
Unsaid needs that play
Within us
In simmering summers,
And winters that say
Hither, love, hold me warmly
Until dawn makes partings
Real. Oh yes persistent caresses
And zephyrs stray

Invocation

My hands have sculpted your face
And they have affectionately gone on
To form you along the torso, and your legs
And returned to sculpt your feelings, your breasts

Yet for too long I have paused,
Your moist exhalations, hot breaths
Of poems, lips that have taught me love
And arrogant pursuits, pleasures

I still wait in the shades, winter echoes
Of snows- white as your marble skin
As I draw in the cloak I know...
Eternity

You know, Aphrodite-
The pages of a scripted universe
Witnessed what I wrote
Between the pauses of kisses
On a chiselled lip

Captivity

Tender steps, hands upon a breast,
You orate, the tyranny persistent
The wuthering windings of haunting desire,
In sallow souls you bring a rose hue,
The sound of a hidden lyre

Yet you become a mist, you pervade gently
Merge inside me, a cavern of dark
Probing thoughts, plying tendrils, arousals
Of the nether mind, a hibiscus in your hair,

A stage set, the strings of petulant notes,
An archipelago of rippled reflections,
The hem of a danseuse's skirt,
And a coiffured head, sunlit lace
In crescendos of magical swirls,
You conquer, you pour out lustre
And the passion, worlds aflame

How deep can you dive into me?
The tango, primordial senses awakened
In whispers of tender words, yet again
My eyes stray on the palm, husky words,
Hush you say, I would take you, eloquence
In the eyelashes hold you in harness

Aphrodite of sunset rays you have arrived
Upon the doors of my evanescence, I fade
As you wax in brilliant lusty invocations,

Perhaps a newer moon from Jupiter's home--
I echo my swansongs in a cavern of stars,

Careless indeed, careless words of dust
Swimming in my skies, the cosmos of red,
Finally the words find a meaning
Voulez-vous coucher avec moi ce soir?
Would you sleep with me tonight?
Sleep is the last thought then... Aphrodite

To Aphrodite- Revisited

In the faraway shores
Inside my heart
You ripple like a wave
Yet bring me the high tide
And gifts, passion,
I feel you, my love,
In this little cosmos
Breathing you, touches
That say you are here

The years have gone by
As you have chosen
The night becomes a cradle
Of rhythms, throbs,
My agonies subside,
Words and your voice
Become the pallet
Of abandon,
The deluge of thoughts
The interregnum of desire
Still like a volcano,
Paused, for the dreams
The finale, eruption
Of insane happenstance,
Erotic lava
Of poems unleashed

Aphrodite, your limbs naked,
White, breasts of roses

As you rise from the sea
I watch the fire
A mantel of cusped palms,
The cup of insane ambrosia
In your lips

Forever you in my mind
A tender adolescent dream
Ripened sometimes,
Yet perennial, green

Solo Thoughts

Without witness, standing alone in the sky of lust
I stare hard, juvenile in thoughts, luminous dust
And kisses of torment in an abandoned love nest
Of orgasmic harangue, stolen in blanched unrest

Avalanches cascaded from erotic montages
I swear hard, give me the soft light, presages
Too arrive with fragrant wisps, and then I choose
My dream's end, a full stop to serendipity in blues

Light fills my sky, desire for fresh breathing flesh
Amour, nocturnes, strident wants, desperate,
The sky turns red on these white hot desert sands
Gently, I pick up my gun; gazelle, stoned she stands

Perhaps she knows- death needs a little loneliness
A few moments to reflect upon love, without witness

MOODS

Unnamed yet

Dreams begin
And dreams end,
Tides too go away
Wet sands remind of yesterday,
Murmurs and shadows softly play,
A rippling brook from another world
Like ivy on a trellis, gently curled
Tendrils softly nudge, nothing said,
You happened, you kissed,
Winter rain. Lovers asleep
So near, yet so far away...

Vectors

Nostalgia is a vector... it points to the unattainable,
You make me sit here, wishing for many things
As the wine warms and you draw the curtains,
As the windows close I watch, I am still here, yours,
Do you wonder about the night- the strange semantics
Of this wait defy me, two sips later, I find emptiness.

I opt to stay until dawn, poems may happen someday
We share the limits of illicit thoughts, inviolate so far,
Harnessed in gentle smiles, passion remains truant
There are pointers that say we may, someday, perhaps
Windows would remain open, when it is summer

Queries

The soul, inside the kernel,
And a kernel inside the soul
Torment begins with existence
And existence metamorphoses,
With these questions
Can I ask how many stars are there?
Do I know if this Universe discovered me
As a foundling?
Or we are both foundlings
Discovering Chaos?

A million questions later, we know
Time has eaten into us,
Gently we turn to dust
In the lifetime of a blink,
Between birth and death
And the miracle of Sapience

And I wonder
Just as you do,
By what name
Or whatever be the name
The soul needs not us...

Kanchan Bhattacharya

Secrets

Phoenix, nauseated perhaps
Of his ashes and poetry like
Its recreation,

Phoenix,
Locked inside the myth
The abundance of life
Tethered to polymorphic thoughts,
A false front
Inside, the fire forever,
The lies
Of the creative wings
Locked in a cage
Survival, reality, fate

Phoenix, my secrets
Of flight
Within this Bohemia...
This polyhedron
Of a glass world,
Echoing unseen
Secrets semaphores
Messages from the Eocene days
Of extinction
In a checkmate

Phoenix, burn gently,
Feel the twirling smoke
Of a long dead cigarette

A microdot on paper
Evanescent life
Crumbling moods

The ashes await-
Arivedersi
When you go…

My secrets stray
Into the air, those wisps
Unshared, forlorn

Rhapsody

When you begin to believe in me
Put your head on my chest
And hear those upheavals,
Those rhythms of a drum
Singing the song of nothing.

Let me touch you and feel this ether
This everything you mean,
This song of crescent moons,
Let me listen to your lips
Singing songs of the wilderness.

When you begin this journey
Put your hand on my eyes,
Let me see then the things I want to see
Those hues and those thoughts
Of touches, of this soul feeling.

Bring me what honey bees seek
Bring me a sip of life tinged with bliss
Bring me back those lost days
Bring me back our sunshine times
Bring me that lost rhapsody…

Dark Love

Rather late, don't ask for bitter things, try
This dark chocolate, as brown as your eyes
Of the wistful kind, in a never time,
That mood and more you leave behind!

Finger tips that walk on lips, the slow kiss
And ah, waltzing alone- anon, just wish
Music- black and brown hits and misses, late nights
By a river side, eyes that sparkle, silver light,

Dark love, in layered folds, words of seduction,
Wary sometimes, yet careless, on the run
Midnight calls and whispers begin again…
Like the time when the moon hides, yes! This rain

Mystery woman, whisper through desire
Will me on, my chocolate lover, fire…

Crossroads of Time

At the crossroads of time, a lonely man
Stands, ponders over his minimal needs
All his life has he struggled, a greedy swan
Picking pieces of gold from his misdeeds-

The last years were rough. Friends were lost so oft,
Weeds grew in his yards. His children adrift
His wife no longer his, his heart now soft,
Whither to? Rather, he wished for death swift...

Such be the man's fort. Once mortar and stone
Fending for himself: years and rough weather
Sometime she thinks, no more, no more of this
His soul now seeks a mate. His weary bones
Amid hills and snow lie his hopes tattered
Yet trudges on this Godless one, seeking bliss...

Going Somewhere

Certainly, not never, nor ever
In between, a million times
Squirming at midnight, I discover a little thorn
Stuck upon my conscience
Unable to tell you, unable to remove the prickly reminder
Of how love is like this estrangement
Of doves in mid-flight, a buckshot of the unfriendly hunter who shoots
Like Cupid with poisoned arrows,
Who cares if I could say my good byes? Who cares-
If you chose the walk along a rail track at midnight
In to the sunrise? Or backwards
Till the final night arrives?

Don't tell me that you were going somewhere-
Nights are paths into dawns and sometimes to the evenings before.
It depends- memories begin and end
Here in the darkness, I wonder about the lingering stars
That fall apart one by one, Andromeda still has losers
That flare into supernovas, we are just going somewhere,
Squirming at midnight, twisting the stiletto
In between, a million times over
Certainly, not ever, nor never…

A Poem of Kisses

So hard to stay away, yet living in a bitter world,
Storms blew out the day, it is always nightfall.
Unkempt, dried out looks, yet fingers so gently touch-
Caress the keyboard, his silence says so much
Pleading with God, his prayer is the piano
He has strange admirers- most he never knows
Beneath cardboard lids, he shivers in the nights
Wonders why God blessed him this gift of delight-

So the kisses arrive softly, melodies begin soft
With black and white strokes, gentle crescendos oft!

Wet January Day

Do you know loneliness like I do?
Long hours, this wait, when my days fade
In the simmering haze... the mists of winter
Waiting in the wilderness, the wind speaks sometimes.

Sometimes it whispers my name, mostly it rests
Upon the notes of a chime, an open door
Where once many stood poised, a threshold
Of hope, now verse has ceased in mid meter,
Echoes too have stopped to tread on the inroads,
Through a portal to dreams, I see the union
Of the skies with the horizon, sunsets,
Ships change their course, oblivious to the SOS,
I wonder now why some choose their end
On isles, I recall the events in déjà vu,
The voices of palm trees and the waves,
Before loneliness makes its claim once again
Without regrets, I remember you, yes...

Moments

Quo Vadis, she asked me

As I rose from the bed of flowers
At dawn, I had spent a moment
Tied down, facing her
And plucking the thorns
And healing the wounds,
And the meteoric showers
Of words and songs
On her lips, and held on
With my octopus grip
Not wanting to let go all,
And she seemed to be brazen
And kept unwrapping her mysteries
One at a time and she was like a tide,
The swelling bride
Of the moon of wanton plunder,
In silent caresses and twisting
Staccato taps on my conscience
As I stole the day, the night
And spring, summer, rains, autumn and winter
Relentlessly in flight
She remained as she was,
Forever beautiful and I
Had to leave Pandora,
She had too many questions
I knew not their answers…
In the last gasps
Of eventide

When the black shadows arrived
She was in her nuptial best
In insatiable ecstasy

Quo Vadis said her smile...

Mantle

A halo, a flaming volcano, a red and amber flow
Those whispers to the breeze, rhymes of love so slow
This is nemesis, a trembling earth, deathward I go
When the throbs would tell- yes, this is all, all I know...

Would you smile? Would you whimper? Would you
For once stand in the limelight of charcoal blazes too?
Your face is dark, aliens on this planet of ashen flue
We have discovered the mysteries of life, we, two!

And so it goes on, Prometheus amid the heavens
Strangers in the night, lyres in hand, flaring incense,
A message of the winds that returns to the seas, in the cadence
Of unsaid subterranean tugs, the feelings of absence...

I wear the mask for one last time, an enigmatic mantle
So eager to exchange words of desire, a lost preamble...

Close Enough

How close am I, Ultimate?
You pass me by,
Meteorite like, in near misses,
You sniff and reject
Those who I wish would die

And then comes my Nemesis
Salvage, save, redo, rejuvenate...

If you ever knew my heart
This vessel of red hate...
Being who I am, I!

Pinned Up

I stare hard at the pin up,
Still trying to decipher the thoughts
Inside a piece of scrap, a letter
Sans life, distance and time,
Ages of agonizing, your whispers died
With your breath at a standstill instant,
What is this pain called, an unnamed blaze
In a forest of images, a letter pinned to the wall...

Although there are lost things wavering in the dark,
Although you choose to remain unseen,
Although I wish you were with me,
The universe is dead, my dreams remain
Twisting in passages in the Sumatran straits,
Poison, I abort reason, treason rhymes

Love is a passage, God intervenes- He smiles
And you whisper, touch me, begin,
You know it is the pain, loneliness
Hot summers, aberrations, perpetuated sin...

Droplets in the Sun

Little droplets, tears of the sun
I buy diamonds, you whisper... just one
Just one kiss- when I go away- a hunter
Running amok, lethal guns.

He hurts me every night, takes me askance
Marriages that hurt, serve or die, severance,
Wanton man-thoughts, sotto voce thoughts
Barely masked, breasts of a woman, not yours.

So you swagger, hello my biceps man,
You cry out, this dream has a collage of hate
Soft once, softer now, and you have poison
Loaded now! Mother fucker... just not fun!

Try and pleasure me, touch me here, and here
Undo my sanity, kiss me- cook me rare
Take me as quick as you can, my areolas bare
I wait, adultery, an affair. Just a night, a flare...

Dragoons charge, you smile, you say "love I am here"
Zeus has his lesser starts, I look at Hera, or Xena, Dionysus
Struggles, you ask this was yesterday, I am ablaze
Take me home, or make one for me... say you care.

I love things, nexus, slithering into my thighs on fire
Droplets, rain, flickering flames, amber desire
My lover innocent, I am a little thorn, and rain
On my flames, quench my soul, droplets insane...

Choose...

Just choose a day
I would acquiesce,
In the evening when the sun sets
And the woman next to me cries

Just choose
What dreams I have, but to change,
The woman in my eyes
May help a lot, with some lies

Just choose
My kisses are the same
At dawn or night,
Even at noon
Nothing at all dies

Just choose the needles,
Thorns and the bread,
The poison the fear,
The gold and the silver,
Black dread, still
The skin erupts, bled,
I would find wings
A few flutters
After few tries

Just choose
Those whispers in the night,
Or the touches in a dark room,

Lips, tongues,
Skin, pats, whatever
Just find just pick
The reason if you must,
Why...

Cues

-I-

I weave,
A spider of infinite patience
Maybe, I miss you
In the outpourings
Of warm summer evenings,
When the loneliness begins
In jasmine wafts

I wait,
Outpourings arrive
In the seismic shivers
Of entanglement,
In the depth of lost times,
And now the rubble reminds
It is time that belies
The dust, the finiteness
Of being there once

I write,
Tell-tales of some seismic sobs,
When the window pane mirrors frosts over
From my moist breath,
The deep lust,
The expiration imminent,
Pirouettes of nakedness
Pivoted on toes,

A woman's kiss
Catapults and tumultuous whispers,
Yes a tango on tiptoes
An aerial pivot

-II-

I console,
The rubble of Time, torn leaves
This day has burnt me
In summer sun, parched, drying
And embers that enthral
The fire of summer,
You made me alive once-
This loneliness is my death,
Urgent, a climax
An orgasmic take off
Whispering needs,
Intimate lips,

A woman,
Infinite hopes clutched to her chest
Her thoughts, cues
To being alive- knowing why

Dark Fire

Every time one has a dark phase
A stage when you feel abandoned
One wonders about guilt and blame
Because nothing seems to be the same
You say never, never, again and again

As you delete memories of a love life,
You perhaps see the stars and the moon
In shades of darkness, amid the moraine,
You can feel abandoned, hopeless
In the intensity of the pain

Walking alone in the darkness
You wonder where she is now
You feel cold and say it is the rain
You know the loss is forever
And you just go berserk, insane

Would you say to the darkness,
How do I go on, do you feel my pain
You wonder why should you continue
Wading through this miserable reverie
Million steps, why again and again?

Don't you want the rain to become a torrent
A deluge from where no one returns
Never, forever, you just want to be alone
In the dark night again?

Burn, burn, burn, don't talk to my mind-
I want to walk into the stars, blazing sapphire
Maybe, like a meteor I just wish to be lit
In the darkened horizons, in a dark fire!

ON POETRY

ON POETRY

Be My Voice

Like the zephyr,
A distant starlight word
Floats across
In a journey of light years
And a path of a million years,
Yet, with your voice
Caress my lyrics
My distant soul, distance
Is a thought-
Just that!

Be my voice
Husky, throaty,
Tendrils to fill my heart
With roar of the stormy seas,
And midnight walks
With the Muse,
The sound of chimes
And the flute

Like the tornado
Rocking this boat,
A shallow coracle
Just two leaves,
Afloat
In the salty spray,
A long night
Lingering in an ocean,
Ripped apart

Kanchan Bhattacharya

Like the rainbow
When you find me
On the shores
Of a distant day...
Be my voice
Starlight Woman
My poem from far away!

Poetry

Sometimes they say gently to no one
Magic lies in translated tactile impressions
Or inked paper, wasted whiles,
Whiskey, rye, rue, faith, love,
Calypso, high seas and storms
Oh yes! Distances and proximities,
Dialogues in incense, laments and death,
Danseuses, exotica, ukulele and flamenco,
Mistresses from the deep sea,
Mermaids and whores, dichotomy

Sometimes the ardent whispers of a drunk,
Begging for a little more of tragic verse,
Sometimes the woman raped, sometimes words like

"Siempre he dicho
Dios te ama
Pero Te amo aún más"

The universe of poets is euphoria,
Of being there- in loneliness, in dungeons,
In distress, in a mess, in amorous bliss,
In a world beset by neverness, broken wings,
Broken nests, a harvest of losses-

I live for you, words that take me away
Far from hurts and burns, I soar, I believe

The language of poets, soliloquys
Imagination, strung in clouds...

"Siempre he dicho-//Dios te ama//Pero Te amo aún más"
"I've always said//God loves you //But I love you even more"

If You Wish

If you wish
This winter to be less opaque,
Take away the mist
And look at the blue sky
Through cirrus wisps and whispers
Of the breeze

And yes-
I speak of myself
Trying to spread wings
In flight
From Siberia to the oceans
Of warmth within you,
Closeted somewhere
On a beach
Or may be, in dark rooms
Where new stories unfold
Amid caresses
Of souls, in tidal waves

Why is it that I always ask
For a beginning,
When every night ends
With a forfeit?

If you wish then
Look at the winter sky,
Pristine cirrus
And whispering winds

Past these windows

If you wish,
Let me lay my head
Upon the heart I seek
Within you

If you wish,
I would sleep
Long enough somewhere
Amid this opaque haze!

If you wish...

Paradise Lost

I stand in this freezing night, looking for flesh, yours...
Scorched by the daemons of love- brandishing the torches

In my mind the eclectic maiden
Ethereal, her lips carving out thoughts of food
Carnal canyons, faraway there is a radiator
Blue flames, she stands, her consort
The flicker of a shadow at her feet
And she gently holds out her palm,
In it, a papyrus of ciphers

The silver moon, barren lover,
A scorching fever, a muted woman
Weaving carnal threads
This loom of desire, the Satan
And Dionysus, His Consort
Eating my verse of the Nether,
Distant flames flicker, a speechless scream
Echoing, in the labyrinthine passages
Runs the lady of destiny, stripped
Of her robes, a crone, her barren womb holds
The secrets of my future, scorched soil
My soul food to her... maggots eating

I stand in this blue haze, Satan smiles
He holds out his hand, he invites
The trident, to his powers, I accede

When the dawn arrives find me,
They call me Milton, he of the lost paradise...

ELEMENTS: WATER

Rain Woman- Sraboni

In rain or in the tempest
Or the heat of summer
On fire

A lost waif, timid
In her rags
Tattered hope
In the hibiscus
Or her lips
As a maid, ready
For plunder

She would soon be here
Amid the crackling rain
Upon a tin roof, afire, yes
She always arrives

Gentle love
Climbing gently
As her tendrils curl
Around me

Rain

March showers from the sky
Tears on my chest
Zephyr, rest your head
In fragrant waves, black cavalcades
Coiffured nest

Water...

I have slipped through
The bounds of her story
And I am now on a row-boat
Called history

Of pathogenic origins
Some one here, please listen
To this thirsty heart now
I need to sip
Water, aqua- my soliloquy
Attempts to console me

Traces, dusty thoughts
Modest offerings
A confession
I hate history
Or hers-

Water flows
Beneath the bridge
And cobwebs
Still span the labyrinths
The rusty chains
Lock out
Carcasses
A million skeletons
Still try to find flesh

Midnight thoughts...

Medieval words
Sorceresses
Chanting
Through my lips–
Absent nymphs
Amid water hyacinths

ALCHEMY

Alchemy

When you whisper to me
I hear the zephyr
And when you touch me,
Incestuous awakenings happen
Amid kindred poets
In midnight urgencies

I know the alchemy
The retorts of rhetoric's
The lusty touches of pretence
I still wonder
Why alchemy is all I am…

Rasping hot breath
Perspiring tendrils
We touch and reach
Into the void between
Where dreams sleep

Sepia moods hide
Reasons that breathe hard,
That fiery dragon that never dies
When the mind teases and ferments

I watch the furrowing

Of sheets- wrinkled love marks
As she sleeps, clutching nothing

The alchemy of being us
Stilled by the gasps
Of spent love!

Whispers

You never asked, neither did I
If the whispers in the next room
Were too loud- ours were…
So they heard us in the delirium
We shared.

I wondered what they would do
If they saw us- cooing
Over the ice cream
On your breasts
Perhaps through the window-
Of chance…

The whispers, gratuitous
Said wipe the white trails
That ran elsewhere,

They stared at us
The statue of entwined lovers,
And the handicraft
Of the thief who ran away with
Our clothes of dust
They called him the janitor!

Once though, they would know
We always whisper when the mice run
In the dark or when the young girl stares

And blushes hard
In visitors' hours at noon...

Whisper my love
Centuries of silence
Must end, sometimes, somewhere...

Truancy

My reply to the echoes
Was to speak my thoughts aloud,
But I closed my eyes, my lips too,
Upon an imagined kiss, yours!

I foundered amid the tiny pool
Lily breasts afloat on a fair chest
Green leaves upon a hidden torso
Become the reminder, that the view remains
As the water cools down,
As strangers sometimes seek love nests...

So we find the stirrings sometimes; deliberate
And opt for playing rampant games
And ravage the ethos
Desire is an eagle swooping in foreplay
We have been in this sometimes-
Déjà vu, wannabe's frolic!

Truancy, demons in a feast of fortunes-
They have met, and seen it
Eyes do not lie; nor does the instinct
Of trying a willing mate and volcanic depths...

Echoes still haunt-
Conscience still berates,
And we set sail-
The straits of Magellan wait
With turbulence and lost maps
Of uncharted seas of fate...

Day and Night

One sees a million women by the day,
Moonlight makes me think of just one...
The amber of sunsets never fails to remind
The darkness ahead has just begun

Soon the ghosts would begin their forays
Those formless memories, now like fireflies
They would flitter amid the sleeping flowers
Stealing nectar, changing truth into lies

The past would begin to raise its head
Beneath the putrid moss, below the stones undead
Moist unseeing eyes, staccato cricket sounds
And the vixen would seek fox prowlers around

Why did I think of the moonlight then?
Whispers in silver light, when none ever happened
The women have fallen asleep, cloistered, in bed
Torrid rains of images, a man once, now fled

A million women have walked past, the streets
Empty, lights of loneliness, only the indiscreet
Promenade, red lights, flashing leather jackets
Wolverine peeps, some animal shivers, wet

The summer moon of the last quarter of adrenalin
A woman trudges home, an erotic breeze of sin
The last of the drunken men stirs, she clasps her purse
A dog barks, the men know the apparition, their own curse

And then the taps of stiletto heels fade away
And the moon becomes a mist, a forest of stars
The quick brown sly fox jumps over lazy brown leaves
Those that barely nod in the wake of a passing car

The night is now complete, the million women
Are asleep, waiting for tomorrow's torrent of light
The ghosts settle for a game of chess, some simply slip in
And become the nightmares, bellowing id, fright

A million women, a solemn world, safe in the day
And nights when the subconscious becomes the alien
From Planet Desire, a vampire mood, moonlit yet astray
A million men, hibernating, in exodus, insane...

Desert

You do know that dream
One that withers sometimes
And flowers in tears
In deserts, just cacti
White sands and water
In a crystal flow
Of murmurs, silence
Begins with sunsets

The night sometimes
Has stars and starlight
Upon heavy eyelids
Gentle breath, yours,
Beyond the dunes
I remain the nomad
A Bedouin looking
For you, your lips
Were like dates,
Sweet, gentle succour
And the little pool
Of amber wishes

When the darkness
Intruded again, this
May be my last song
The bird seeks a nest…
Yes this is a desert
Your foot prints lead away

CANNABIS

Cannibals Hate Cannabis

Cannibals are people that keep us indoors
Cannibals want to burn the cannabis store
Cannibals keep us on the ground
Cannibals wish we never be found
Cannibals hate the lovely weed
Cannibals are people I hate to heed...

Cannibals hate Cannabis, QED
We hate cannibals you can see
Let us sing, sing for cannabis
It will keep us in moody bliss
We will be happy and never cry
In quantity it makes us really fly
All the cannibals on this Earth
Have been looking to kill all our mirth
And they make laws that have flaws
Smoke the pot to break their claws

Cannibals hate Cannabis, with that we can argue not
Cannibals are people who do not give pot a shot
In my life I have never done it
I am a cannibal if you think of it
For I love to write of Cannabis
For I love the seedy haired little Miss
A lady who puffs away all the day
I think of cannabis- 'twill make me stray...
I want to hit the high, and walk on the roof
To smoke the pot, to keep smiling, keep aloof!

Cannibals hate Cannabis, QED
But I am a cannibal who loves the weed
Exceptions, you know, do prove the rule
And people who smoke pot are really cool!

So friends don't you wish-
Cannibals must love Cannabis!
I left pot for all my sixty two years
If I think of that, it moves me to tears...

Mary Juanita

Lyrics of a different kind
Somewhere inside my closeted mind
I look for her
In the nooks and corners
I left far behind
Never
Thinking that she would take me
In my brain
She is smoky
She is ethereal
Sometimes
To be shared
She has a broad mind
She enjoys lips
And she drifts
Hangs in everywhere
In a hookah joint
Tempting
To take all
A death wish
In her niche
In bed
Pulsing
The roof comes closer
The mind sees
Things from the Nether
And bliss
It is indeed Miss
MJ
I am here…

I yelled hard
    Not to be seen...
                I got a whiff of her!
Endearments-
    That was her habit
        So I shed a little-
Ash
    That was a hit!

Maria came

Sigh...
        I got high
       Too late in my life I knew
      It was Miss Maria I
     Loved to do
     In the noon
(And croon?)

At night
    It was my Juanita
       As I called her
        Awesome
       Sweet
    When there was light
   Even,
     Maria...
       When sad was my plight
      No

Her name was Mary
   Juanita
     You bought me delight
    Mary Juanita
     A pretty one

     Like Cleo, Cleopatra
    Conjoined
      Carpet clothing
       On the torso within
I loved your- Ahhhhhhhhhhhh!
  Paper dressing
     I loved the way you could
      Take my fingers
Messing

Rolled in a romantic mood
     Into cigarette paper
Your domain
Puff! Puff! Puff!

I am insane
Lit by a matchstick
Puffed hard
Marijuana
Mary Juanita
Yes
You always

//
Hit my brain!

Kanchan Bhattacharya

Weeding Out: Cannabis Haiku

This year will be good
If cannabis sets the mood
For reaching the sky

I love cannabis
Miss Mary Juanita is
Good, I do promise

I began to smoke
When I was a baby bloke
Heavens! Look at this

One puff, and I smiles
Two puffs inside me I smiles
Three takes me ten miles

So Miss Mary says
These are just your pleasure days
Illegal always!

I smoke it enough
So life is high a little tough
Just like making love

Maria gives me grass
She says- smoke cannot just pass
Both from nose and ass

Legalize ganja
We will live better, promise!
Marijuana Miss

Rarely understood-
Smoking pot when in sad mood
Makes it right- too good!

Cannabis is bliss
Unlike hooch, no hangover
Smoke is good, you wish

In the end, I must say
Mary Juanita will always fix
The worries we have
With weird but merry tricks
One can drink and die of cirrhosis
And of OD or more with narcotics
But grass will make always you smile
With simple yoga and Aeronautics!

LIMERICKS & FUN

Limerick Day

I fear that old Mr. Ed Lear
Was very certain limericks tear
The muscles of the stomach
Badly tickled, they're racked
And then made to shake with laughter, it is clear!

A limerick is a poetry trick
That smoothly drops a brick
On the reader's head
With things rather not said
And then whacks the buttocks with a stick!

We have Ogden Nash whose poetry
Was funny, that we can see
But the nutty fruitcake
Was his just to take
When "The puma had no huma"! Said he

I would like to add that no limerick
Is complete unless it makes one very sick
Upbeat that he or she
Would very quietly
Hit the poet's belly with a stick!

Like this…

A sophisticated maid from Delhi
You must have heard this, really
One who would fold herself,
And roll into the kitchen shelf
But surprise… she folds herself into a brolly!

A Nose Is A Nose Is A Nose!

My nose takes the cake for God's sake-
I have a sharp nose
A Roman one, a romantic one- a classic one… neatly done
By Mom and Dad, not too bad, I say-
To the mirror,
You have a nice nose, and pray!

I ask her- "Dear, describe your twin holed
beauty- a diatribe to it is your duty
I prompted her- "Upturned?"… "Ha!" she said!
And I asked "A thing of beauty-
"Like the beak of an eagle- or, the snout of beagle?"
She said "Hey Muse, don't overdo- I differ from your view…
Mine is just a nice nose, really Caucasian, imported, perhaps Russian
Or Balkan, or Prussian, but a nose- carved in marble, perhaps Italian,
Soon, when we marry, we cannot tarry in intent
that elegant statement, heaven sent!"
Your nose, my nose and our nose- an over
dose I thought- she asked-"What?"
I agreed, better than a flat nose on me, said she- "Tee-hee!"
"Oh yes! You mean a nose for everything?"
Well to the ferret, even a pierced nose with a ring is rather boring,
In fact as bad as a betrothal with a sting!

Pensive, she said, "You have a romantic nose, rather close
To your brain, one that drives me insane,
No wonder you can blow- like Moby Dick, you are sick!
To wit, go stick a rose, into your Roman nose"

That's it! Oh, now I know, a rose in a nose is not a rose!

GYPSY

Gypsy Mind

Pathless hunts,
Like Orion on the wilderness
Of tinder heath

Homeless for eons,
Hovering on wings and talons
A bird, a banshee sound-
An intoxicated crescendo

No dreams to dream,
Nor reason to see
Yet entwined
Yang, whispering yin
Orgasmic in creation
Let me alight
Let your chest of secrets
Become the tragedy I seek

Bring me my hemlock
I beckon the chaos
Seeking my waxen wings
I am the Bedouin
Walking milky skies
Looking for Artemis

Dire Straits

Your kisses surprise me
It isn't the time though,
For goodbyes last too long.

A contour in a sunlit window
Twisting and pirouetting,
Stretches my imagination
Mostly like a gazelle about to flee
Into the desert shrubs.

I like the mosaic
Of gooseflesh, memories
Of misty poems in your eyes,
There is a little mountain
Clothes and shoes
Hurriedly left behind in the hall.

Your kisses still surprise me
We have just said our galloping
Welcomes at dawn
Tumultuous, wild
Flesh eating flowers
In a tropical mangrove
And aching echoes engraved.

If you leave midway now
Remember the pungent urges,
Nailed furrows you leave behind
In dire straits, yet to dry

Skilful Lies

At seventy-seven, more or less
I profess
I have met that woman,
That asks for short poems?
An elegy to her happiness
That vanished in making
A piece of evidence
A work of fiction,
An afternoon in a hall
Where people believe
Sincerely, the stains of love
Are wiped out from the mind
My lies pander...

Lies are important
Ego wise, an essential ingredient-
To please and to seek pleasure
One can always profess love
And be sure he means
Nothing at all,
Just for the sake of that kiss
Even a touch of her breasts,
Casual encounters
I add, of the third kind

Lies bring peace, a fabrication
Of détente- I cheat, she does,
In our own way we all do,
The fabric becomes well knit

The gaps get filled in
Till we believe lies are
So help us God, the truth
With floral print and the dye

She sat with me for long,
An hour and a half into the darkness
We discussed
Why we lie to people,
But under oath to each other
We smiled and held hands
In denial, I had a woman for long,
And she, her pleasures
In a disco, where arachnids explore flesh
And hashish delights her mind
We lied and kissed away,
Rather absent-mindedly

Even this is an escape
The truth is actually pulverized
In a food processor's blades
Terminated, with orange juice
And lemon blended,
Just wishing that signal
On her face would say yes

I am skilled at what you too are
Masking my injuries, faults and scars
With skilled presentations
A tableau of lies

Geisha Story

The body of what I do,
Gentle provocations-
Those touches, intrusions
Raising the impossible in you,
Geisha moods
In a paper room
A flickering candle,
The wisdom of light

The shades and delights

The folds of a kimono,
Layers of pancaked skin,
Rouge, hyacinths, blue on white,
Scintillating lures,
Flamenco, cabarets,
A red evening show

A tinge of sorrow,
As you weave webs
And orgasmic flows
In the aftermath,
You gently seduce

The body then turns
Upon petals crushed beneath
This turmoil of twined souls,
This limpid cool

I have seen the bait
The finesse of abandon
Infernos and labyrinths
You tease, entertain yet,
Knowing there is no us
And no tomorrow.

The body of what I do
Is a goodbye
Poised at the door
Of a new dawn
Wants, yes, wants
Evermore

Acid Love

We are on the edge
Doubts begin.
This fall, is too deep
No belaying. No seeds
No stones to fall, no scree.

Love is an acid. It eats me.
Encompasses my mind
And it is the alcohol I seek
From the flask, you pour it
Into my limitless thirst.

Acid comes from your breasts,
Indeed it melts my soul and skin
You permeate.
Acid comes from your lips
That elevating stir,
You stand on tiptoes
And yes, elixir.

Acid love- denials
When I seek to part you
To seek more,
Much more…
And even more!
The serpents and octopi
Slithering
In distress
Let me suggest

Crystal walls, mirages,
Uncharted passages
On stormy seas,
Billowing sails,
Leaning into the waves
Decks awash-

Acid love,
I seek the charred dreams,
Dried flowers folded into diaries,
And awakenings
In midnight ado.

Port and Cognac

I know nothing of wine,
But just my women and whiskey, sublime,
Serenade me, said she, slithering, lissom, tresses,
And traipsed in, my tipsy muse, black, black dresses...
With her came temptation, a gypsy, calypso beats
Seduction entered too through a dark door, neat
Serpentine whispers, a suggestive entrée
Of delights, missing were those kisses, pleas...

Dissolved in the bubbly, frothing fireflies aglow
Dimples, breasts. Flamenco, I asked? No, she said, think tango,
Rasgueados began, fingers ran through her hair, red wine, claret eyes
In tempered rhyme, she spoke- a woman needs your poems, your sighs
I smiled and asked, oh, the wine?
She smiled, inside my heart, yours to find...

Winter, I stand knocking, cognac strands, a mewing kitten, a shawl
Wrapped around her fair shoulders, perhaps to bare if she falls
Whiskey lips, none knew the Muse, except, my eyes found the words
In common time came the aria of thoughts, wind chimes, guitar chords

A cellar full of memories, a drunken bard, inkpots, quills
Woman of conquering eyes, port of call, a thrush sings, trills

WOMEN

The Mysterious Me

Things never change, do they?
So we hired out that shack
Painted it... blue, red, white and black
Then, like lovers always do, lost our way...

Woman, I think we made a pact.
Mondays we would walk the marble paths
The Cosmos is a small place. Mondays are Tuesdays
Confused through until Sundays

Things never change. The Sundays of cakes
Wading with the ducks, a tour through the lakes-
Sunday- I believe you like. Then there are the weekdays
Where dreams ferment- smile in red green black greys

Things never change. This is foreplay
In my clichés- my days are made of soil... clay
Of my heart, of my soul, of my night, my day
Tell me of weekends. I love you, I say

Bring me some latency. Hide me, cloak me in mystery
When you read me, be my voice of dreams that I see

Diary of Death

She wrote two words

                    Everyday

            A chronicle of how

        From chrysalis to butterfly,

          Came this journey

          Amid white clouds

           Blue skies

           Green earth,

        A day is all they have

She spent the day,

A day

A day

In her garden of love

Of the ink stained sky

When it rained

Into her heart

        At the edges of the rainbow

         Into the pots of gold

          With withered wings

           Asleep,

         Into the night

         When moths fly

         And lie

        In death,

        Amid red dawns

She spent the day,
Staring hard
At her line of life
Inked by thoughts
Of narcosis

A diary
    Undressing herself
                Before the mirror
                Before the flame
A night...
A night,
Beneath the stars

        Beneath the roof
          Of despair
          Of life's lies,
        Whimpering cries

A question to the Muse... why does she transit between the chrysalis stage to the butterfly, why is she so transient...

97

Spiced Mutton

Kosha Maangsho, passionately cooked
Spiced and dried meat, if you wish
We would walk down. Take a metro ride
To Fatehpuri or Chandni Chowk
And I would smile
When you rub my shin
While looking at the menu
Staring blankly, at the biryani
While I stare merrily
At the full breasts and smells of curry
Floating past me in a hurry

We may walk. Burp. Shop for that OTG
And come back to f**k after feeling the heat
Inside the warm shop, eager to admire
The fire within us… Oh, the fabled OTG
Hungry, really hungry, for that spiced meat
Like your breasts, windswept hair
Rouged cheeks

Dried aftermaths, a white towel
Swaying in the sun
Kosha Maangsho! Whisper to me
You wanted to make it
Like we had it last night

I have a tooth ache now,
Kisses and love bites

Palindrome like beginning with Kosha
Yet again, admirable, this gluttony

This New Year
Clad in tuxedos
Waiting to eat time
Alcohol turns to urine
And a baby beggar smiles
That's all in a while...

That man ran out of time.
Those lovers in the restaurant
That tree of Time
Kosha Maangsho arrived

The Fly

Destined to love, so destined to fail,
I tried to watch the fly on its trail

The fly on her chest is blessed with many things
Fandango and other dances, sometimes wings

And I stare hard- a million memories it brings
Sigh! Fly, go away, white chest, too many wings

The fly is here on honeyed words
The fly is flying, fingers on guitar chords

Destiny is for insects that make it good
And woman, you kill me, just as you would

Oh Fly, just fly away, this woman won't have my say
Oh Fly, you can't rest, on that woman's white breast

Don't make a sound... it is out of bounds, o fly
Oh Fly, just fly away, let me swat you... and I lie

Oh Fly, just fly away, this woman is a big dream
Naked by the creek, naked always, and so it seems

Destined to love, so destined to fail
I tried to watch the fly on its trail
Destiny is for insects that make it good
And woman, you kill me, just as you would

Atrium

I dunno if it was poison...
I dunno if it was a kiss
Between and betwixt, of course,
I loved your lovely lips!

Upon shallow seas, barrier reefs...
Talk to me when my dreams have ended
Tenderly ever, have you asked me, hear...
If those lips brew ambrosia?

Dream of me not, I asked
Of those vagrant thoughts
Impaled upon thy lips
Were the portents of causes lost?

There were chasms, examined,
There were perchance those wicked dreams,
Whence love was taken askance of-
We lost hither our wisdom, brimming over at the seams

I dream, thy navel in those tips
Of talons- I forsake thee amid the fire
Leave me or love me, my Muse
Thereupon ends a saga of blues
Atrium?

A hell to which we were born
I have lived through the desert
And borne **** many a scar,
All the unforgotten sighs of scorn
To just be absent from thy love, forever shorn…

Monochrome

Little by little, over nights
This forlorn censored terminus
In strange rooms

If there is shame in this
There is hope,
Escapes into danger,
Silver lined clouds'
Sunrises, and yes
Promises of hell,
Blessings of the Satan
Just these invocations
Of all they can,
An erotic zone of kisses,
Mushrooms in full bloom

Monotony, monogamy,
Monorail harmony,
Maniacal distress
More shades of Destiny,
Faded roses, whispered wants,
Agonized intervals,
Adulterous hormones,
A niche of negatives,
Monochrome souls.

Candid surrender
Facile, tender, gentle
Desert, oasis
In sunset

Night

Oh Yes!
Nestle gently. Make me beg
For a few gasps of life
Amid oregano rhymes of lips,
And spasms, volcanic times
Overflowing along red flames,
Soul to soul in midnights
Of rains, be naked
As you always promised,
On my easel of blue
Between the sky,
On the river of inflamed desire,
Where then would you be?
What would you choose to wear?
Sundays make me long for so much
And you smile...
Beginning my verse of darkness
Of temporal love,
Folded into rolls of memories
With thyme and salts of fabled times,
I have long ago admitted
This salt, the pepper
Of my agonized love,
Seems to say yes
To never before dreams
Of unsaid words...
A woman of unknown tresses
Her face veiled in mornings,
In a dream of mists

Wrapped in nimbus,
Gently wet, little dripping twigs
And entwined tendrils born
A little messed up,
This passion,
This hope of someday,
Amid mushroomed soil
A bed of clay,
So many things to say
Oh yes… if?

Neutered Midnight

Beyond the small strains
Behind the wasted stolen looks
Lies a sullen silence
A woman, voiceless

Her small hands, once soft
Now lined with chalk and ashes
The stains of burns
She cooks
Sometimes, being her man's urn

A blank mirror-
A close up of her Spartan waist
Almost vanishing birth marks
A pair of still proud breasts
An image
Ravaged by her husband's sex
And by that black shame
That suckled children
Longing desire
Her loins full of fire
Mellowed in uneven cobbled pathways

She hides her eyes
Her life lit by fireflies
And a million lies
When you look into her eyes,
You see her agony
And the crow's feet of a wasted life

In her mind lie neatly folded dreams
And ironed saris
Handkerchiefs and faded blouses
Tomorrow she would work again
Teaching children
Eating her lunch
Until of course
Beneath that red evening sun
She begins her walk back,
To that man, listless
He hates her
And she hurts

To count her steps
To leap into the sun
She would perhaps dream of that lost passion
And the billowing poison moon
Of a neutered midnight

Castle

It is hardly the time
To feel the pangs of-
It is hardly the day
To find you are-
It is hardly the year
To know that something is-
It is hardly the life I need
Missing you
Gone
Not right

The canopy of time
Segmented in spectral pieces
Strung on the spines
Of an umbrella
If I loved you
I would have
Found the minute
The hour
The year
The life
So the wheels turn
Spin, dizzy
In the rain, as I
Open my palms
And stare at you
Silhouetted behind
The closed door

In the portico
Where memories
Are memorized
And cleansed
I stand beneath
The open sky
In ruins

The castle
Crumbles
We hold out
Unaware
Our breath merges

POTPOURRI

POTPOURRI

Confluence

A time, sunlit
Stirring in the noon,
Nights would bring
Stilettos tapping,
Windows holding out,
Pine cones
Frolicking in the snow
In moonlit dales.

When will I sleep?
Winter is a time
When the aches begin for spring,
When whispers and cobwebs
Hang in limbo
In a room of poems.

Poison loiters in alleys
Of strange thoughts,
Standing listless, but still...
Waiting for the keeper of keys,
The Muse and Death
Passions of verdant greens.

Slip in,
Put your palm into mine,
In this prison,
Dawns and nights
Locked in greys,
Take me-

My hemlock love
Afloat in eddies
Of this confluence
Of midlife streams.

Ingress

You do wonder, don't you?
Where this path leads to,
And the road is winding, he waits
Beyond the bend, and listens
For your footsteps
And you blush, "perhaps!" you say
He may, and he smiles, says nothing,
A poem on a piece of paper
His thoughts for a petulant day

You wonder don't you- he says so little
But asks so much, inside you
You see a trail, hidden beneath
Mists, silent thoughts reach across
And set you astir, and the stirring says
Yes, he is not opaque, he stays,
Just a whispering page
Of ceaseless caresses, a swirling
Chanced upon tornado,
Needs and agonising waves

You still wonder, a month has passed,
He has not returned, an ambience lost,
There was a dream, there was this wetness
Of teardrops, dew like on a blank page
A mirror sans an image, a crystal ball
Tinsel caught in eddies, nary a face!

Haiku of Life

A hand-rickshaw, shade,
Asleep, just water his meal
And his dreams loiter,

Green louvers, hot sweat,
Red bricks, summer sun, dark clouds,
Mistress of Park Street

She would go home, hers
He smiles, not his, but just bread
Easy fare, she too sweats

Night and day they pass
Like anytime machines their days
Of agony, rape

A poet's silent lap
The muse's trousseau of whispers
Beneath wet skies, blessed

Park Street, dreams and love
Yesterdays, whiskey, sex, nights
And a canyon deep

Soul of an Officer and a Gentleman

We are your freedom fighters, my countrymen...

He who never came back
What would he say?

Panic begins
Meet my soul, walking palm groves
All yours, my breath, my gasps
Begin the refrain, soul
My will upon these twisted ways
Wanting you
Gently,
Wanting you all the way

So ask me
Once, in ellipsis- just once
When I am gone,
Remnants of that scent
That essence of love
A taxi ride
Climbing into the hills
Noon to night
Delight, touches
In a wet room and soggy wet beds
In an Army mess...

Dreadfully, when I am gone
Into the meadows
Into Elysium

Dreadfully dead
Laid low and hurt
Going home
Going home,
And gone on a day,
A rainy day
When the floods came,
Ashamed
Because this is not going to be
When I am gone,
When the marigolds are black,
I would miss you
Till who knows when...

Guns say it all...
Have been firing all day,
My child, and yes,
My woman, you are safe...

He who never came back
What would he say?

Death of a Marriage

Prosaic moods-
Of alienation,
Of crisis,
Auguries, maligned

Night arrives
With a pall of moody rejections,
The man becomes himself,
She cries, agonized, utilized,
Despised...

A rusty pan
Some tea leaves
And a spoon
In the man's lips
Doubling as a spade
To extract
His buried future

A day again gone by,
The sunset remains
In the distant past,
Wrapped in the junkyard
Where spat out love
And semen
Sprout a seedling,
Black mushroom blooms

Metal Hues
Sepia colors,
Listless, on move forever,
A beginning to an end
Monotonous access
Into brittleness

Bard's End

Which strand of The Bald Bard's hair
Wooed which woman, I ask thee, Milady Fair
As is the plight of many famed men of verse,
Perhaps by Hamlet on the walls of Elsinore cursed

His beard white, a bit too much of it on his short
stature- his mouth- muffled by the critics...

On his manifold points of wit secured
By the dazzle of his Muse, deeply lured
The Muse, much used, now indignant, yet scared
Shrieked aloud... brace thyself poet, you DARED?

The Bard is a menial. To evil intent

On the path to doom you are set
Your poems are like the cockroaches
Upon the caffeine in decrepit bistros,
Scenic phraseology- obscene, sans stated remorse

He writes in his own way this bard- emeritus seduction

Bard- your poems kill me. Muse says she is on the lam.
Doors closed. Windows bring in the miasma of love
Penetrating silence ensues. Death happens on a bed of woes.
No one winds this clock. Eons ago, it ceased. Closed.

Ode to My M

The unsaid things
Ripe, sexed
Far too many on which life is silent
Whispering zephyrs
How does one say what needs to be said,
For what blossoms inside
The flower of dreams,
Waiting in the ides of hearts,
If poems be like you my love
I would be the forever poet

Tourmaline and topaz
Crystal from the deeps of the Earth
Beset in papyrus rolls,
Thus be you
Asleep in my arms
When it rains,
Or be in the shadows tall,
As I stand over you in the sun

I do dream,
I do have hopes
Of a midnight moon
Beneath the stars,
And silver lochs
Host to a million thoughts
Of a pan of gold
Diamonds and the rest,
Rainbows you know best

Evanescent Moon

Poised at this window
The city of mirages beckons
The volcano in it flares,
Memories sometimes storm

The citadels of lust,
Spires reaching high, like breasts
Red thirsty lips
The bees, the birds in a cuckoo's nest

Pour me honey, I ask
You smile and erupt, lava and kisses
In the netherworld of loins
Touches, tendrils, serpents, hisses

The night becomes a liquid
Millions of throbs pleas, this heat
The metronomes of sweating vales
Merged, beating in resonance retreat

Can this be Utopia on Earth?
We have chosen this night, this tar
Of passion on us, all over writ

Poised, this clandestine home
Removed from the bed of poison
We cling, feelings on metal rails
Gently we smile, treason done,

We wait, entwined, we know
We would do it once more,
We begin the chants again,
We can wait, delights in encore...

Evanescent moon... thin,
Setting in the west at midnight
Then we are left with the loneliness,
Just the loneliness of starlight

Sea Shells

Three days was all I needed, but then
She got it all wrong, it was a death of pride
I came to tell her it was good bye,
Nothing more…

But there are many things that happened,
Was she trying to tell me the same, the same night?
Love was a happening
Sunk in whiskey and a freak out

The sea has a line of hotels
Laden with salt and illicit will,
Eyes burn, the spray,
And she knew some how
The sea-shelf was wide
As I tried to tell her, and lied

The sea roars, this wetness
I stand on sand
Looking for seashells,
The crabs run up into my shorts
And remind
It was never that she wanted me,
But she loved the sea
Inside my mind

Sing me those songs
Mermaids smell
Of passions

Sell me seashells
And I would hear the words of faraway shores,
I limp at times,
Though I plead to all
If it shows, never show you know,
This sea is deep-
Just wade
Till I die,
Just pride, you know,
Just pride!

Rancour

Suave morons
A tottering nation
Of halfwits who chose their destiny
Now find their bliss in being have-nots,
The change they sought
Has come to naught
The flavours of sops
Go to the haves,
The twists of yarn and rule
Behind the masks

Looking for the ass
That works for me,
These animals
Live not long
In popular fancy,
The dream of lucre
Entices all,
And the plebeian
Pays

Drunk as a pig
On hard hits
Of travesties
Of illicit laws
I seek to revive
A bit of the honour
That once belonged to me

Kanchan Bhattacharya

In the summer sun,
In the torrents of rain,
Shivering in hovels
You find
The sinner has sinned again,
Looking for food,
Looking for life
Looking for soul
Morons…

The River

I live gently, breathing softly,
A pulsating stream,
Hoping, smiling, dreaming...

A peep into your eyes-
Dark mist,
A blue seeping sky-
Your thoughts
Cascading like a distant waterfall.
Once upon a time,
It was a cloudburst,
A torrent of torment,
A spiralling carnal event...

This anticipation is mad!
You loiter, choosing the kind of evening you want to happen.
You pirouette and smile, a song on your lips.
You are the undoing of all time to come.
I look at you, and my eyes gleam.
I reflect the coming darkness of the skies, and I am the stream.
I am the image you may sometimes touch.
Gently, you would stride in, seeking me over
you, rubbing me upon your skin.

Touch me- I am ready too, as you wade into my
body, my sand banks holding you up.
I know you would swim, and kiss me, as I flow over you, dreaming.
A union...

You know me now, flowing full in these monsoon days- the river in spate!

Rattenfänger

The wisps were like the dragonfly,
He wrote with the smoke, a sigh...
Many times over, I love you!
And casually blew arrows through
The hearts he puffed, into the faces
That glanced and traced
His movements, ah! So passionately profiled
And then Peter gently smiled,
He said he was a traveller,
A Traveller of Time, not a town dweller
And the poor girls knew not he had lied,
But to touch him- and to be touched they tried
Then the innocent man took out a guitar
And sang a song that took their hearts so far
They sat there, caring not the state they were in,
Peter, Peter, they wooed him, until sin,
And he sat there smoking his stuff
With his blue, white, green and grey puff,
Blowing into smithereens many a heart or two,
And the maidens did what he wanted them to do

Peter then meekly begged to go
And the maids said, not so early, oh no!
So they sang on and he played
For sixty nights and as many days,
Soon the merry girls felt they had to go
And tell their mothers they were at the Peter show,
And a baby would come along soon
Coz they were affected by the morning swoon,

And then Peter went off through his Time Machine
And the poor girls remembered the story of Hamelin,
And there was a set of girls who had vanished,
And the rest were praying, he should be dead, they wished,
But Peter, the Catcher of Rats, appears again and again
Elopes with women enchanted with musical strains!

In a new domain, six dimensions apart
Peter now handles a pan, at a super-mart
His four women, they admire their man
And are glad him they could understand.

(Rattenfänger... The Rat-Catcher)

Life Time

Life is indeed complex, me, you, he, she, they and them!
Pronouns and hesitations, nouns and action!

Once the shadows begin lengthening
Like now, we surmise beneath those greys lie
Hidden meanings, transposed callings
Birds seeking home, nestlings praying
And darkness begins the envelope, night
Seeks the day's amber rays, then the stars

We seek the pronouns. We hesitate. We capsize
Like sail boats with a mad man at the helm...
We arrive into the pronouns, transformed anew
Into rose buds on lapels, caressed, admired and dumped
I say I was, you were, he was, she, perhaps and they left
Shadows, mirages, cornucopia unwarranted love, dust

We seek the nouns. Those blooms, gardens of ardency
The aromas, the yellow grass flowers, the dahlias
And we know, we have to begin something. Action
Steal, pluck, kiss, wish, yearn, drink, love, kill
The shadows grow- we want the light- windows
Claustrophobia, seeking an escape, the dawn

This is a shadow zone, Pandora smiling in shades of grey
Pompeii on the edge, the water, lava, pumice, malice
Images negated, browning out, ripples, dancing dark waves
Time ebbs gently, the nouns fall, the pronouns hesitate

Flamenco Night

Dusk came on tiptoes
Seeking appeasement, zephyrs
Caressed and vanished,
Then came the musk, her tresses
Brought new messages urgent

She spoke of nothing,
Scattered notes of Beethoven
Appeared on her lips

Souls metamorphosed
Amid the dews, uncertain
Silent communions
Surging crescendos, gentle soft
Dulcet moonlight peeping in

Who cares if the night
Never appeared in this room
Of delight afire?
Flamenco abandonment,
Elfin smiles, dereliction

Bidding my goodbyes
As dawn arrives, gathering
Fragrance, her longings,
Ivy amour bade adios
At the doors of a chateau

Epilogue

Where my poems speak
In tired voices
Of longings unfulfilled,
Pencil sketches that remain
Unfinished, incomplete
Stories buried in metaphors,
And yes, whispers sublime
Tell me to close my eyes
For the final mile-

Change, says Time
For the wind blows harder, harsher
Each day of life gets colder,
And aches grow shadows
Roses still fragrant shrivel
On gravestones,
And the Muse pales
A tremor in her voice
Of denials

When you know the final gasps
Weave the last wreath
And lay it
On the snow,
My last poem must say
Remember me never,
But the sea of words
Would bring the salt
Of tears, I let go

My epitaph is a rose
Carved into the earth of rhymes,
When you recite through the blue skies
And I lie in my shroud of green,
The thorns, shimmering sunbeams…

Printed in the United States
By Bookmasters

Printed in the United States
By Bookmasters